# Boon-doggle

A book of
**LANYARD**
**& LACING**

*by the editors of Klutz Press*

**KLUTZ**®

Development:
Ann Zerman Sanders
Anne Akers Johnson
MaryEllen Podgorski

Design and Graphics:
Elizabeth Buchanan

Renderings:
Ellery Knight

Instructional Art:
Teshin Associates

Page Production:
Elizabeth Buchanan

Interference Throughout:
John Cassidy

Table Top Photography:
Pete Fox

Photo Credits:
Page 13: "Creature from the
Black Lagoon," Courtesy
of Motion Picture & TV
Photo Archive
Page 18: Harry Houdini,
Bettmann Archive
Pages 23 and 46:
Lifeguard, FPG

Published by Klutz,
Palo Alto, California.

Book manufactured in Korea.
Boondoggle and accessories
manufactured in China.

*Write Us:*

Klutz is an indepen-
dent publisher located
in Palo Alto, California,
and staffed entirely
by real human beings.
We would love to hear your
comments regarding this or
any of our books.

**KLUTZ.**
2121 Staunton Court
Palo Alto, CA 94306

## Additional Copies

If you are having trouble locating
additional copies of this or other
Klutz books, give us a call at (415)
857-0888 for the name of your
nearest Klutz retailer. Should they
be tragically out of stock, additional
books can be ordered from our mail
order catalogue. See back page.

4  5  8  5

ISBN 1-878257-72-2

# Cool Stuff to Make

# Introduction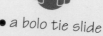

Most of what you'll need to boondoggle is already attached to the book, but there are a few things you'll need to round up on your own.

## What We've Included:

- boondoggle
- a key ring
- two lanyard clips
- a bolo tie slide
- a metal bracelet bla

## Other Things You May Need:

- scissors
- glue (Elmer's Craft or All Purpose Tacky glue work best. You can find these at craft or fabric stores.)

- clear fingernail polish
- Scotch tape
- a paper clip
- a big clip
- beads and buttons

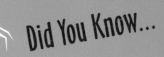

## Did You Know...

★ *The art of boondoggle can be traced back through the cowpoke craft of lasso and halter making, which is a form of braiding using four, six or eight strands of leather...*

★ *Boondoggle owes much to the art of splicing and knot making as practiced by sailors over many centuries...*

★ *The art of braiding itself goes back at least 500 years.*

# BIKE STREAMERS

*You will need:*

- twelve 2-yard strands of boondoggle
- a pair of bike grips

**1.** Make a loop of boondoggle and feed it through your grip. Use it to pull the streamers back through (hook them in their middles).

Loop

**2.** Then get rid of the loop, tie a knot in the middle of your streamers so they don't all pull back out, and pull it into the handle.

**3.** Repeat with the other bike grip. Put your new grips on your bike and HIT *the* TRAIL

# Braiding Basics

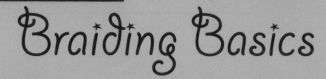

● THE STRETCH: Before you begin, straighten your boondoggle by grabbing it in your hands and "stretching" it.

● THE ANCHOR LOOP: Boondoggle braiding is much easier if you anchor one end to something you can pull against as you work. We favor the "loop over knee" system. Make an anchor loop by cutting a piece of boondoggle about 24 inches long. Before you start each project, we'll tell you how to hook this strand onto it. After you've done that, you can knot it into a loop and slip it over your knee to pull against.

Don't have any knees? Tie your loop to the arm of a chair, or loop it around a doorknob.

You can use the same anchor loop over and over.

● THE ALL-IMPORTANT FOLD: It's important that you <u>fold</u> each strand as you braid. Fold like this:

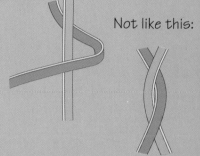

Not like this:

● NEATNESS COUNTS: You'll do best if you hold each strand of boondoggle close to your work, being very careful to keep each in the right order.

● Stop every once in a while and pull each strand down and out to the sides to tighten the braid.

● To keep really long strands of boondoggle from twisting and tangling as you work, wrap the end of your boondoggle into a little bundle, as shown, and tie around the middle.

# DIAMOND BOLO TIE

*This is called a diamond bolo tie because the boondoggle braids into a diamond pattern. Decorate the slide with a massive real diamond if you can. If you can't, use a button, charm, fake jewel...*

## YOU WILL NEED:

◆ four 2-yard strands of boondoggle (Just use two different colors for now. We've used green and pink in our instructions—it will be easier if you start with these colors too.)
◆ a bolo slide (it came with the book)
◆ something to decorate the bolo slide
◆ two beads (optional, but nice)
◆ glue

**1.** Before you start braiding your boondoggle, glue your diamond (or whatever) to the bolo slide and set it aside to dry.

**2.** Hold the four strands of boondoggle together and tie them in a knot. Leave a couple inches of boondoggle hanging free.

7

**3.** Slip two strands of boondoggle through the anchor loop.* Pull on them so your four strands are nice and even. Arrange your boondoggle exactly as shown, with two pink strands on the left, and two green on the right.

**Original knot**

← **Anchor loop hooks over knee**

**4.** Start your braid by folding the <u>outside</u> right strand (it should be green) <u>behind</u> the two inside strands...

**5.** Now find the outside left strand of boondoggle (this time it will be pink), and fold it under the two inside strands...

...then fold it to the right so it crosses <u>over</u> the inside pink strand and becomes the new inside green strand.

...then fold it back to the left so it crosses <u>over</u> just the inside green strand and pull it tight. Now this pink strand will be on the inside. Confusing, isn't it?

**\*If you don't know what an anchor loop is, look at page 6.**

8

Repeat steps 4-5 until your bolo is at least 25 inches long or as long as you want it. Be sure to leave a couple inches of unbraided boondoggle at the end.

**6.** If you're using beads, thread all four strands through a bead, then tie all the strands in one knot to hold it. If you don't have a bead, just tie the knot. Trim the ends so they are about an inch long.

**7.** Untie the original knot to get the bolo off the anchor loop, then finish this end just like you did the other end in step 6.

**8.** Slip the bolo slide onto the braid as shown, and you're ready to go.

**Back view**

**TIP:**

**I**f you have to leave your boondoggle before you're finished, you can tape the strands down on a piece of paper in the right order. If they get all mixed up anyway, pull the pink strands to the left and the green to the right. Look at each of the outside strands. Whichever is higher is the one you start with next.

# Spiral Bolo

You can make your bolo a little different by braiding the boondoggle into a spiral design. The only difference between a diamond and a spiral design is the order in which you arrange the colors at the very beginning.

Again, start with four 2-yard strands of different colored boondoggle. We've used pink and green.

**1.** Start just the way you started the diamond braid, with the four lengths of boondoggle attached to an anchor loop. Spread the strands out so they look exactly like the picture.

Original knot. Untie it when you're all done.

Notice that this time the colors alternate: first pink, then green, then pink, then green.

**2.** Now braid just like you did before, being careful to keep the strands in the right order. First, fold the outside <u>right</u> strand under the two inside strands...

...then fold it back to the <u>right</u> over the nearest strand.

# 3.

Now fold the outside <u>left</u> strand under the two inside strands...

...then back to the left over just the nearest inside strand.

Repeat steps 2 and 3 until your bolo is at least 25 inches long or as long as you want it. Then finish your bolo by knotting the ends and attaching the bolo slide, exactly as you would do for the diamond bolo.

**T**here are tons of things you can use to decorate your bolo slide besides massive diamonds. Look around and be creative. Don't rule out any small decorative item—tiny toys, pieces of old broken jewelry, fancy erasers, seashells, nice buttons, charms...

# FISHY ZIPPER PULL

*You can attach this fish to the zipper of a jacket or backpack for a really* **SNAZZY** *zipper pull.*

You'll need two different colored strands of boondoggle, each about 4 feet long. We've used blue and pink in our illustrations. It'll be easiest if you use these colors your first time through.

**1** Start by crossing the two stands of boondoggle at their centers. In our illustration we've crossed the pink boondoggle <u>over</u> the blue.

**2** Fold the top strand down.

**3** Now fold the left strand over to the right. Make sure your boondoggle looks exactly like the illustration before you go on.

**4** Fold the right blue strand back up.

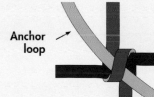

**5** Now fold the top pink strand <u>over</u> the nearest blue strand and under the farthest one. Check the picture— it will help. Pull all the strands tight.

You should end up with a nice square knot with a piece of boondoggle coming off each side.

**Anchor loop**

**6** Turn the square over so you can see the bottom. Slip your anchor boondoggle through one of the diagonal pieces of boondoggle, then tie the anchor in a loop and hook it over your knee or a doorknob.

**7** Turn the boon- doggle back over. Easy.

*YIKES! Don't stop now!*

**8** Now fold the top strand down and the bottom strand up (both are blue), making sure these two strands don't cross each other.

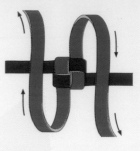

**9** Cross the left pink strand over the blue strand that is nearest it, then under the one that is farthest away.

**10** Do the same thing with the pink strand on the right: cross it over the nearest blue and under the farthest blue strand.

**11** Pull all four strands tight, and you've finished your second knot.

Repeat steps 8-10 until your braid is about 3 inches long.

**TIP:**

This is a good way to hold all the strands in one hand.

**12** Now it's time to make your braid into a fish. First take your anchor loop off. Then fold the braid back on itself as shown.

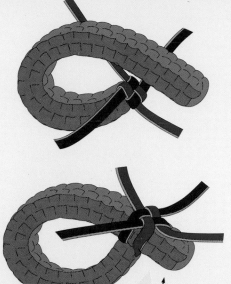

**13** Make another knot right on top of the braid you've folded over—just like you've been doing. Pull this knot really tight to hold it in place.

Tail fin

**14** Continue braiding until the second tail fin is almost—but not quite—as long as the first one. Pull all four strands tight, divide them in two, then tie them in a good tight knot.

**15** Tie your fish onto the zipper of your choice, then trim the ends.

15

# KEY CHAIN

You probably shouldn't try this one unless you've already learned the diamond braid (page 7) and the square knot (page 12).

YOU'LL NEED:
two pieces of boondoggle, each 4 feet long, and a little Scotch tape. We've used purple and yellow boondoggle for ours.

Tie your anchor boondoggle to a key ring (we've included one with the book), then tie it into a loop. Slip your boondoggle through the ring and center it so that you now have four strands of boondoggle all the same length. Make sure the colors are arranged exactly as shown.

**All four strands the same length**

16

**2.** Now fold the right strand _under_ the two inside strands...

...then back _over_ the inside yellow strand.

**5.** The next step is to change from the diamond braid to the square braid that you used to make the fishy pull. Hang on.

Start by tying the two inside strands together in a single knot. Pull all four strands tight. This is a good time to take the anchor loop off.

...then _over_ the inside purple strand.

**3.** Fold the left strand _under_ the two inside strands...

**4.** Repeat steps 2 and 3 until the braid is about 10 inches long.

**6.** Arrange your boondoggle so that it looks like the illustration: one yellow strand pointing away from you and one toward you, and the purple strands pointing to the left and the right. They won't do this naturally, and it may not look too neat at this point, but don't worry about this.

**9.** ...and weave the right purple strand over the nearest yellow and under the second.

**7.** Start your square knot by folding the top yellow strand down, and the bottom yellow strand up.

**10.** Pull everything tight. You should have a nice square knot.

**8.** Then weave the left purple over the nearest yellow and under the second...

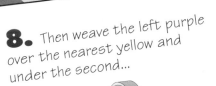

**11.** Make another square knot in just the same way, but this time leave the knot pretty loose. Be sure your strands are neat and you can still see the shape of this last square knot even though it is loose.

**13.** ...and pull it far enough that you have about 3 inches of finished braid coming out of the top of the square knot.

3"

Pull everything tight.

**12.** Poke the ring and finished end of your braid right up through the center of this knot...

**14.** Now continue making square knots <u>around</u> the finished section covering it up until the square section is about an inch long.

**15.** To finish the square knot, you have to tie a special finishing knot. Before you start this knot, make sure your boondoggle looks exactly like the illustration. If it doesn't, tie another knot and it should look just right.

Leave your last knot a little looser than usual.

Check the illustrations if you get stuck. They make more sense anyway.

**16.** To finish, you're going to wrap each strand part way around the knot, then pull them up through the center of the knot. The arrows show where each strand goes. See the next page to find out exactly how to do this.

**17.** Start with the bottom strand. Loop it under the right strand, then poke it under the last knot and up through the center. Don't bother pulling it tight yet.

**19.** Loop the top strand under the left strand, poke it under the last knot and up into the center.

**18.** Now loop the right strand under the top strand, poke it under the last knot and pull it up through the center.

Keep going no matter what ➡➡

**20.** One more and you're finished. Wrap the marked strand down then tuck it up under the bottom part of the last knot and into the center with the others.

This one

**21.** Hold the square braid in one hand and the loose ends in another, and pull it all really tight. Trim the ends at angles and you're ready to go.

*The classic lifeguard lanyard is made just like the keychain, but* **LONGER.**

# *Classic*
# LIFEGUARD
# LANYARD

Better not try this until
you can do the diamond
braid (page 7) and the
fishy pull (page 12).

*Y*ou will need:

- ⚓ two strands of boondoggle, each 3$\frac{1}{2}$ yards long
- ⚓ a lanyard clip (we've included one with the book)

Attach your boondoggle to the clip,
and work the diamond or the spiral
braid until it is 28-32 inches long
(it has to be long enough to slip
over your head when the two ends
are joined). Finish the lanyard just
like you did the keychain (starting
with step 5 on page 17).

Clip a whistle onto the lanyard,
and **GO SAVE SOME LIVES!!!**

KEEP OFF

# Wrapped

## HEADBAND

*You will need:*

- 2 yards of boondoggle
- a plastic headband
- a decorative button
- tape and glue

**1.** Tape the end of the boondoggle to the inside of the headband, near one end. Angle the boondoggle as shown.

**2.** Begin wrapping snugly.

**3.** Continue wrapping until you come to the place where you'd like to put your button. Thread the button onto the boondoggle and position it at the top of the headband.

24

**4.** Finish wrapping the headband.

**7.** When the glue dries, trim off the end.

Glue

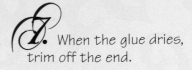

**5.** On the inside, use an unbent paper clip to gently loosen the last few wraps.

If you like, you can dangle a few charms off your head-band. Cut two 10-inch lengths of boondoggle. Tie these around the stem of the big button already on your head-band (leave the four ends of the strands dangling). Slide a small button into your desired position on the bottom of each strand. Tie a knot below the button to hold it in place, and trim the end at an angle.

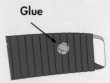

**6.** Insert the end of the boon-doggle through the last few wraps and pull it tight. Dab on a dot of glue to hold the end in place.

Pull tight.

# Woven Bracelet

### You will need:

✖ a flat metal bracelet blank (it came with the book)

✖ nine 10-inch strands of boondoggle in various colors

✖ 4 yards of boondoggle for wrapping

✖ tape, file, crochet hook, scissors, glue

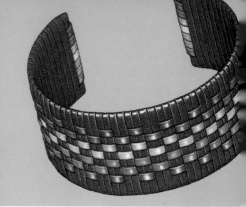

**1** Use a file to smooth the edges and corners of the metal blank. A metal fingernail file is great.

**2** Arrange nine colored strands* side by side, on a piece of tape so that the tape is about 1 inch from end of strands. Keep the strands neat and close together.

**Tape sticky side up**

\* We're using two alternating colors here—it's an easy way to start.

**3** Carefully center the metal blank on top of the flat strands...

**Back view**

...then fold the ends of the tape down to hold it together.

**Front vie**

26

Glue

Back
view

Front
view

**4** Fold one end of the flat strands around to the back side and tape it down. Slip the end of the wrapping boondoggle under the flat strands. Secure it with a drop of glue.

**5** Begin wrapping around the blank, covering the flat strands. Wrap seven times. Check flat strands to be sure they are lying flat; don't let them twist or overlap.

**6** Lift five alternating flat strands.

**7** Wrap twice; push wraps snug to previous wraps.

**8** Lay the five strands back down, then lift the other four flat strands.

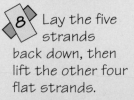

**9** Wrap twice and push snug. Pull flat strands tight.

**10** KEEP IT UP! (Repeat steps 6-9.) Continue to lift five alternate flat strands, wrap twice, lift the four other strands, wrap twice, etc. Keep everything nice and tight.

**11** End with seven full wraps.

**13** Push the end of the wrapper boondoggle through the flat strands.

**Back view**

**12** Use an unbent paper clip to gently loosen the flat strands at the end.

**Back view**

**Trim this end at an angle.**

**14** Pull the boondoggle tight, seal the end with a dot of glue, let it dry, and trim it.

**Back view**

**Glue**

**Trim as close as possible.**

Curve the metal band to fit your arm. Curving around a rolling pin works great!

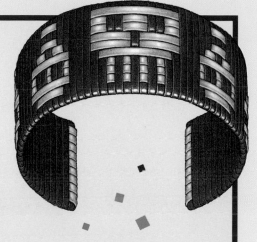

## Make up your own designs:

**O** n a piece of 1/8-inch graph paper (it's the regular kind), mark off a section 66 squares long and 11 squares wide. We show a few examples on the following pages —you will have plenty more ideas of your own!

## A few design tips:

**1.** It's a good idea to start your design sketch in the center of the bracelet and work out to the ends.

**2.** Allow at least six rows of squares at each end of the design for your beginning and ending wraps.

**3.** Each strand must be held down by a wrapping strand at least every **10** squares; otherwise, it will be too loose.

**4.** Follow the graph design by alternately lifting and covering the weaving strands (the ones that go the long way) with the wrapping strand (the one that goes the short way).

**5.** As you weave your bracelet, keep your place on your graph paper design by placing a ruler under the row you are weaving. Move the ruler row by row as you complete each step. Turn the page to see some samples.

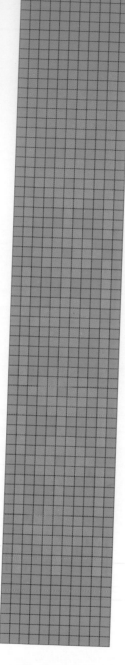

### Skulls

Try this design using glow-in-the-dark boondoggle!

### Southwest Star

### Lightning Bolt

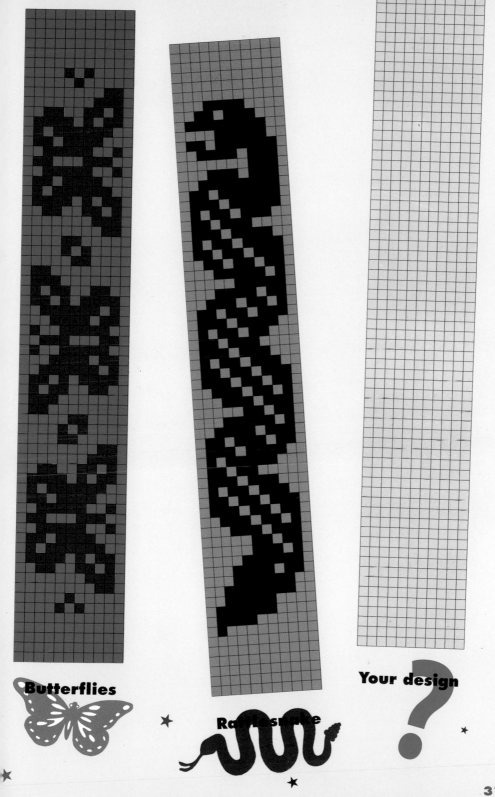

**Butterflies**

**Rattlesnake**

**Your design**

# *Wrapped* BARRETTE

You will need:

- 3 feet of boondoggle*
- a plain metal barrette
- tape, glue, a paper clip
- a decorative button (one with a fat stem on the back)

**\* If you want a fancy fringe — two 9-inch pieces of boondoggle, four (or more) beads or buttons**

**1** Start at hinged end of barrette.

Tape end of boondoggle to inner side of barrette.

**2** Wrap the boondoggle around the barrette, pulling it tight and pushing each loop snugly against the previous one. Go about halfway.

**3** Thread the button onto the wrapping strand of boondoggle, then continue wrapping to the end.

**4** On the inside, loosen the final few wraps (use an unbent paper clip as a poking tool if you need one) and push the end of the boondoggle back through. Pull it tight and put a dab of glue to hold it. When the glue dries, trim the end.

## If you want to be *Fancy*

To add fringe, cut two 9-inch lengths of boondoggle. Tie the center of each piece around the big button.

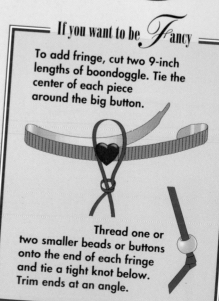

Thread one or two smaller beads or buttons onto the end of each fringe and tie a tight knot below. Trim ends at an angle.

# Woven Barrette

You will need:

- ✖ a 3-foot piece of boondoggle
- ✖ three 7-inch strands of boondoggle
- ✖ a plain metal barrette
- ✖ tape, glue

**1** Lay the three short strands flat down the middle of the barrette. Secure at the hinge end with a bit of tape.

**Tape**

**2** Tape one end of the long boondoggle to the inside of the barrette, near the hinge.

**Tape**

**3** Do seven wraps, tight and close. Then lift the center flat strand and do one wrap over the outside strands*.

**4** Now raise the two outside strands and do one wrap over the center strand.

**5** Continue to wrap, alternating strands to get a checkered pattern. Keep the wraps tight and close together. End with seven plain wraps.

**6** On the inside, push the end of the boondoggle under the last few wraps. (An unbent paper clip helps.) Pull it really tight and put a drop of glue to hold it, then trim off the loose end.

**Glue**

**Pull**

**7** On top side, remove tape and glue each end of the wrap. When glue dries, trim off excess flat strands.

**Glue**

**Glue**

**Trim**

**Trim**

*If you've made the woven bracelet on page 26, you're already familiar with this technique.

**33**

# Snake

This braid starts out just like the braid you used to make the fishy pull.

**YOU'LL NEED:** 1 yard each of two different colors for a 5-inch snake. Plus, a little bit of pink (tongue) and two small beads (snake-eyes).

**1** Cross the two strands of boondoggle at their centers, making sure the pink strand crosses over the black one.

**2** Fold the top strand down so it ends up looking just like the illustration.

**3** Now fold the left boondoggle over both of the black strands.

**4** Check the illustration to make sure your boondoggle matches, then fold the bottom right strand back up over both of the pink strands.

**5** Now fold the top pink strand over the nearest black strand and under the farthest one. <u>Pull all the strands tight</u>.

34

**6** Turn the knot over so you can see the diagonal piece of boondoggle on the bottom. Attach your anchor here, then tie your anchor into a loop.

The anchor loop will be used later to make the snake's tongue, so choose a good color.

Up to this point, you've started just like you did for the fishy zipper pull. This is where the twist comes in.

**7** Turn your knot so that the pink strands come off to the left and the right. Fold the top strand (it's a black one) down and to the <u>left</u> of the bottom strand.

**9** Now weave the left pink strand <u>over</u> the nearest black strand and <u>under</u> the farthest one. Make sure this pink strand crosses the center at a diagonal and ends up in the bottom right position (check the illustration).

**8** Fold the bottom black strand up and to the <u>right</u> of the top strand. Both of these strands will cross the center at a diagonal, but they don't cross each other.

**10** Cross the right pink strand over the nearest black and under the furthest. Make sure this strand crosses at a diagonal and ends up in the top left position.

**11** Pull your knot tight and repeat steps 7-10 until your snake is about 5 inches long. Leave at least 3 inches of loose boondoggle at the end.

**TIP:**
This is a good way to hold all the strands in one hand.

3" or more

**12** To end your snake, you have to tie that special finishing knot. Leave this last knot loose.

You're going to wrap each strand part way around the braid, then pull it up into the center. The arrows show where each strand goes. The next few steps show you exactly how it's done.

**13** Wrap the bottom strand of boondoggle under the right strand, then poke it under the last knot and up through the center. Pull it all the way through but not too tight.

**14** Now wrap the right strand under the top strand, poke it under the last knot and up through the center. Again, don't pull this strand too tight.

36

Keep going!

**15** Do the same thing with the top strand, wrapping it under the left strand, then up through the center.

**16** There will be one strand on the outside left. Wrap it part way around the outside (see the arrows in step 12), then poke it up into the center through the last knot as shown in the illustration.

**17** Hold the last knot in one hand, the loose strands in another, and pull everything _really_ tight.

**18** Trim the ends short at the bottom of the braid, then trim the anchor loop short to make a tongue.

Trim the anchor loop at an angle.

**19** Tie a thread around the two pieces of tongue to hold them together, then glue small beads on to make eyes. If you don't have beads, you can draw eyes on with a felt tip pen.

Thread

**The End!**

# Spiral Bracelet

*You'll need two pieces of different colored boondoggle, each 2 yards long.*

**1.** Start this one as if you were doing the snake braid (page 34). Follow the instructions on pages 34-37, but this time make your braid 6-7 inches long. The braid should be long enough that you can make it into a circle and slip it over your hand.

*Pull tight.*

**2.** Once the braid is as long as you want it, cut the anchor loop off and pull all four strands really tight.

**3.** Separate the strands in two as shown...

...then slip two strands through the loop at the very beginning of the braid (the anchor loop was just here). An unbent paper clip may be a help. Pull these strands all the way through so that both ends of the braid are touching.

**4.** Tie these two strands together with the other two strands, pulling everything <u>really</u> tight.

**5.** Tie one more tight knot, then trim the ends off.

# *Adding* CHARMS

**Y**ou can make a charm bracelet by threading buttons and whatnot onto your boondoggle as you braid.

You'll need some shank buttons (check the illustration) with holes big enough for the boondoggle to pass through.

**1** Just before you start a new knot, thread a button onto one strand.

**3** ...then tie your next knot. (In this case, we're still making a spiral knot.)

**2** Push the button all the way down so it is close to the braid...

**4** Push the button down to the side of the braid and pull the knot really tight.

Make at least a couple of knots before you add another charm.

**You can use longer strands of boondoggle to make a necklace in the same way.**

# Shoe BOBS

**You will need:**

- two 40-inch strands of boondoggle
- eight 6-inch strands of contrast color
- two large beads
- a pair of shoelaces
- scissors, clear nail polish and a jaw clip

**1.** Take one 40-inch length of boondoggle, trim the end straight, and wind it into a tight coil (see tip on page 42). Keep it smooth and tight.

**2.** Trim the outside end at an angle.

**3.** Hold the coil with a clip and coat half the back of the coil with clear nail polish. Let it dry, remove the clip and coat the other half.

Jaw clip →

**4.** Thread a 6-inch piece of different colored boondoggle through the center of the coil and tie a knot on the ends. Pull the knot snug to the outside of the coil, then trim the ends at an angle.

**5.** Repeat with three other 6-inch strands. Be sure that one of the knots catches the end of the coil.

...then center the bead and the coil on the shoelace.

**6.** Thread a bead onto one shoelace. Push the shoelace tips through the center of the boondoggle coil...

Your shoelace →

**7.** Repeat the entire process for the other shoelace. Now you've got a pair!

# C☉SMIC earrings

**YOU WILL NEED:**

❨ two 2-yard pieces of boondoggle

❨ two 11-inch pieces of contrast-color boondoggle

❨ two nice-looking buttons with shanks

❨ two earring backs (from craft store)

❨ nail polish, clip, scissors, glue

**1** Take a 2-yard length of boondoggle and trim one end straight.

Begin making a tight coil.*

**2** Keep coiling until you have a circle the size you want. Keep it smooth and tight.

Trim the outside end at an angle.

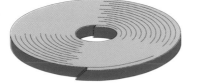

**\* Pinch the boondoggle in one hand between your thumb and forefingers and make a tight coil by turning it between your fingers. Use your other hand to wind the end around the center.**

**3** Clip the coil to hold it flat and coat half the back side with clear nail polish. Let it dry, then remove the clamp and coat the other half.

**5** Check to be sure button is centered, then pull the ends of the boondoggle even and tie a knot at the edge of the coil, pulling it tight and close to the coil. Be sure the knot catches the end of the coil lace.

**4** Make angled cuts at both ends of an 11-inch strand of some contrasting color. Thread one end through the button,* around the outside of the coil, up through the center of the coil, through the button again and back through the center of the coil.

**6** Trim the ends of the knot at an angle.

**7** Glue the jewelry fitting to the back side of the earring.

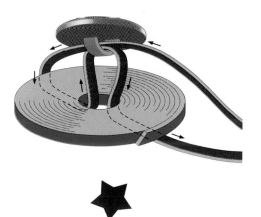

**\* Button has to be bigger than the hole at the center of the coil.**

# Rosebud Pin*

**YOU WILL NEED:**

✿ ten strands of boondoggle, 10 inches long, in your choice of colors

✿ a pin back

✿ tape, nail polish, glue, clip, scissors

Before you start, stretch your boondoggle to make it as straight as possible.

**1** Stack ten strands of boondoggle in a smooth pile. Arrange colors as you wish.

**2** Wrap a piece of tape close to one end of the stack.

**3** Curve the bundle of strands into a loop, keeping lace smooth and tight. This can be a little TRICKY! Work carefully and patiently. You can use a clip to keep the strands in their proper order.

\* This one takes patience. Don't try it until you have a little boondoggle experience.

**4** Put one end through the loop. This is the hardest part. Don't give up!

**5** Pull the strands tight one by one, starting with the innermost strand.

**6** Hold the loop in place with a clip. Coat half the back side of the loop with clear nail polish. Let it dry, move the clip and coat the other half. Remove the clip after the polish dries.

**Pull TIGHT!**

**7** Take the front bundle of strands and finish each strand with a tight little knot   looks like a spray of flowers! Trim ends to desired length. Remove tape.

**8** Glue the pin on the back.